My Personal
Poetry Photo Book

(Honoring & Celebrating)
Family

Book #1

By: Precious Won

PALM HANDS PUBLISHING
Corona, California

For information on speaking engagements, poetry readings, theater performances, and to request the author to attend or perform at your event visit the website or email at:

Email: Preciouswontheauthor@gmail.com
Author's website: Preciouswontheauthor.com

Instagram: PreciousWonThePoet

Amateur and professional performances of
this series (Book #1, #2, or #3)
must be obtained from the author in writing.

This book series is available to colleges and universities at quantity discounts for bulk purchases.

Library of Congress Control Number: 2021905222
Won, Precious
My Personal Poetry Photo Book #1 (Honoring & Celebrating Family)
ISBN-13: 978-0-578-68998-2 (paperback)

Meet the author at: PreciousWonTheAuthor.com

Subscribe to: "The Precious Won Poetry Show" on YouTube @ThePreciousWonPoetryShow

My Personal
Poetry Photo Book
(Honoring & Celebrating Family)

My Personal Poetry Photo Book is a wonderful keepsake which allows you to place your fun, special, and memorable photos to go along with the heartfelt story and poetry in this book. Your book will be personalized because you get to choose your family photos.

Come honor and celebrate important and meaningful people in your life, as you enjoy this story of a family's love and their triumph of family unity.

What People Are Saying:

"A touching and wonderful story about family."

"Precious Won brilliantly weaves her poetry into a heartfelt story about family. Her poems flow into the story like perfectly orchestrated music."

"I loved the poetry in this book. It was not calculus, Greek or the Morse code. I didn't have to read it five times to understand or decipher it. No complex riddles, or a difficult puzzle to put together, it was simply beautiful literature that I could relate to and enjoy."

"A much-needed book. Refreshing, enjoyable, and meaningful!"

"My Personal Poetry Photo Book (Honoring & Celebrating Family)" by Precious Won, is a creative and beautifully written poetry book of a family's love, tragedy, redemption, and triumph! If you like Lorraine Hansberry's "A Rasin In The Sun" you will enjoy this book about a family's desire to keep their bond, strength, honor, and love for each other."

WHAT IS YOUR FAVORITE POEM IN THIS BOOK?

Leave reviews and comments about your favorite poems by subscribing to:

"The Precious Won Poetry Show"
on YouTube @ThePreciousWonPoetryShow

Visit the author's website at: preciouswontheauthor.com
Coming Soon! (Book #2 and #3) in this series

DEDICATION

This book is dedicated to families across the world. A family is a special unique treasure.

We love God, we love ourselves and like a cherry on top of a sundae there is also the love, joy, and blessings of family!

Family

A family should stick
together like glue.
Never let anyone
break the bond of
family for they
will surely be blue.

Honoring:
Honor thy mother
and father, so your
days may be long.
Never disrespect them
lest you'll be
singing a sad song.

Awards & Accolades:
Despite your awards and accolades
never forget the love of family,
and don't throw them shade.
Always remember it was
from your mother and
father that you were made.

Celebrating:
Celebrate family, for
family is a special gift.
Hold them close to
your heart, be grateful,
forgiving, and uplift.

-Precious Won

CONTENTS

INTRODUCTION...1

This book is designed to be read page by page. The poetry intertwines with the literature herein.

Poems by title in the order of appearance, Book #1

I. HONORING:

Mother

1. *A Mother's Love*...4
2. *Somebody*...8

Father

3. *For Father*...12
4. *A Man*..15

II. AWARDS & ACCOLADES:

Husband

5. *Forevermore*..39

Wife

6. *Our Love Poem*..42

III. CELEBRATING:

Son

7. *A Good Son*...55

Daughter

8. *My Lovely Daughter*...59

Grandparents & Grandchildren

9. *A Grandparents Love*.......................................63

Friends

10. *A Friend Is*..68

Acknowledgements……………………………………………...90

Discussion Questions…………………………………………91

Page of Fame Honoring & Celebrating Family……………92

Family Tree…………………………………………………...96

Bonus Family Journal………………………………………...97

About the Author

My Personal Poetry Photo Book

(Honoring & Celebrating)
Family

Book #1

CHARACTERS & AGES:

Ryan: (Main Character, 35)
Mother: (Ryan's Mom, 60)
Father: (Ryan's Dad, 60)
Lisa: (Ryan's Wife, 32)
Davis: (Ryan's Son, 11)
Johnathon: (Ryan's Son, 5)
Rebecca: (Ryan's Daughter, 7)
Nita: (Ryan's Daughter, 4)
Kendra: (Ryan's Youngest Sister, 22)
Tasha: (Ryan's Middle Sister, 25)
Lady in Red/Rhonda: (Ryan's Oldest Sister, 28)
Calvin: (Ryan's Younger Brother, 24)
Tammy: (Calvin's Girlfriend, 24)
Kelly: (Ryan's Niece, 9)
Courtney: (Ryan's Niece, 10)

Edith: (Ryan's Mom's Best friend, 60)
Saxophone Player (Male)
Saxophone Player (Female)

ABOUT: Family is important, and Ryan wants to make sure his family bond is cherished. Turn the pages one by one and meet the main character Ryan and his siblings, Kendra, Tasha, Rhonda, Calvin, and other important family members as they take us on a journey into their lives. A touching and invigorating story about family that includes poetry.

HONORING – Does Ryan's siblings believe in honoring their parents or will they let **AWARDS & ACCOLADES** go to their head? **CELEBRATING** family is what some of the family members believe, but unfortunately some people are ungrateful and don't appreciate the blessings and special gift of family. Will Ryan's family keep their close bond, or will it be broken?

INTRODUCTION

The lights are dark. The lights rise up slowly and are dim. The curtain opens and we see a woman playing the piano. The spotlight then picks up on a man named Ryan who is singing along with the piano music. Ryan is the oldest of five in his family. Ryan and his three sisters, Kendra, Tasha, and Rhonda are honoring their mother and father at a theater they rented out for a family event called "Honoring My Parents." His parents are seated in the front row dressed in purple, looking royal. Family members and friends are also at this special event. Ryan's younger brother Calvin is not in attendance. Ryan is singing a song to honor his mother. He finishes the song and bows his head. The soft blue and lavender lights picks up on him. He lifts his head and reads the poem "A Mother's Love."

I.

HONORING

(Honor thy mother and father, so your days may be long.
Never disrespect them lest you'll be singing a sad song.)

Mother
(HONORING)

A Mother's Love

A mother's love is sweet,
unique, true, and
one of a kind!
A love like hers
on this earth you
will never find.

It's hard for a mother
"to stay in her lane"
and that's only because
she doesn't want to
see you in pain.

She will try
to protect you,
it's an instinct thing,
and when you do well
it makes her heart sing!

She will love you
more than anyone
on this earth,
and she sacrificed
her life when she
gave you birth.

A mother is there for you
through your ups and downs,
your laughter and
your frowns.

She will check on
you to make
sure you're okay
and is never too busy
or selfish with
her time or day.

A mother is a queen, special,
and nothing or no one
can take her place!

Her love will live
forever in your heart
and will never be erased.

(Ryan begins to walk off stage after he finishes reading the poem "A Mother's Love." As Ryan is walking off stage his youngest sister Kendra who is a ballerina comes on stage and takes his hand. They join hands and raise them up together in an angle. They both say in unison)

Ryan and Kendra: Honoring*! (They both freeze in position and the lights fade down slowly. The lights come back up and we see only Kendra. The music begins and Kendra performs a beautiful dance which is a mix of jazz and ballet. After she finishes the dance she bows and says)*

Kendra: "Mother you will always be honored, loved, and never disrespected. I dance my heart out to you!" *(The lights shine on Kendra in the shape of a lavender heart. Kendra bows again, and a woman enters on stage with a lavender and blue flower in her hair named Tasha. Tasha is the middle sister. She takes Kendra's hand and they both spin around in a jazz turn and say in unison)*

Kendra and Tasha: Honoring! *(They both freeze in position and the lights fade down slowly. The lights come back up and now we only see Tasha. The spotlight is on her and she reads the poem "Somebody")*

Somebody

Somebody told me,
Somebody showed me,
Somebody helped me,
until I could help myself.
Clothed me, fed me, loved me,
and taught me to love myself!

Somebody kept me safe and warm,
held me within their caring arms.
Taught me to have self pride,
and to be strong,
shared with me knowledge
and taught me right from wrong.

Gave me encouragement,
and said to my dreams always hold on!
Told me to be tough, have faith
hard times won't last too long.

Somebody taught me to love, and to forgive,
taught me the importance of family
and the special bond between friends.

Taught me to help my fellow man,
never be phony, and to be
the person who I really am.

This is somebody special
I love so dear and true.
I dedicate this poem
from my heart to you.

(Tasha bows her head after she reads the poem "Somebody." She raises her head back up and freezes in place with her hands together over her head. A lady enters on stage wearing all red named Rhonda. Rhonda is the oldest of the sisters. She was given the nick name "Lady in Red" by her family because she likes to wear red and it's her favorite color. She associates the color with love. Rhonda walks out elegantly and freezes next to her sister Tasha. Tasha takes the lavender and blue flower slowly from behind her ear and places it in Rhonda's hair. Tasha then dances in a smooth wave motion and exits off stage)

The Lady in Red /Rhonda: Tasha that was lovely! We're also blessed to have a great dad! Sometimes men can get a bad rap about fatherhood. I know it's a lot of good fathers out there. Dad you're my superstar. You were there for me in my bad and good times. You helped me through my first heartbreak and gave me moral support when I lost my job. You also walked me down the aisle when I found my true love, and you encouraged me to start my own business! I will always honor you. *(Rhonda reads the poem "For Father")*

Father

(HONORING)

For Father

This is for my father,
a true dear friend.
This is for my father,
who stuck with me
through thick and thin.

This is for my father
who loved me
and cared so much,
a strong man with a
soft and gentle touch.

My father always helped me.
He was always around.
My father lifted me up,
when my poor spirit was down.

Yes this is just for you,
and all the terrific things you do!
For your encouragement, guidance
and all your love and kindness.

It's not a Grammy, Tony
or a special award,
it's just a poem
saying I love you,
you're the best
dad in the world!

Yes a poem just for
you father…
Love forevermore.

(After Rhonda reads the poem "For Father" She bows and a light picks up on her in the shape of a star with the words father. Ryan walks on stage)

Ryan: We do have a wonderful dad sis! That was a nice poem honoring him.

Lady in Red/Rhonda: Thanks, and I meant every word of it. We have an awesome dad. He is supportive, wise, and kind.

Ryan: You know sis, our life wasn't always easy. We had ups and downs, good times, and bad times, but daddy was always there. He was the king of our family and our mom the queen. They always found a solution to our family problems and the two of them stuck together and made it work. They made problems fall like dominoes.

Lady in Red/Rhonda: *(Chuckles with glee and in agreement)* So true my brother Ryan, so true! They always found a way to make things work. We had such great times growing up, and we still do! Our dad is a hero in so many ways. I'll see you this weekend at mom and dad's house for dinner.

(Rhonda waives to her brother Ryan and exits off stage)

Ryan: *(He waives good-bye to his sister Rhonda)* Yeah, I'll see you later. *(Ryan begins to walk off stage quickly and then freezes in place center stage)* He looks to the left and then front facing. Before I rush off I too want to honor my dad. My dad is also my star, my hero! He was there for me and my entire family! He's always encouraging. I refuse to bash or belittle him. There is no money or nothing on this earth that would ever make me do that.

My dad always told me there is a price for everything in life, but whatever the price may be, never pay for it with your soul or manhood. He taught me so much! He taught me to be a man! I will always honor and appreciate my dad. I want to dedicate this to him.

(Ryan faces the audience and reads the poem "A Man")

A Man

You were tough on
me at times, and
now that I'm
older I understand,
dad you were only
teaching me to
be a man!

You said "Life isn't
always about fun.
You have to learn
about work and
sacrifices my son!"

You taught me
to savor the
good times, and
to deal with strife.
You instilled in
me knowledge and
gave me good advice!

You gave me lessons,
more valuable than
any present or gift.
Words of wisdom that
kept me adrift.

You said, "Son always
do in your heart what
you know is right,
because what's done
in the dark will
surely come to light!"

"All money is
not good money.
Don't be a slave
to it and fold.
Sometimes you need
to leave the money
on the table and walk
away from the gold.

There's nothing worth
losing your dignity
manhood, or soul!
Remember God has
the last word,
he's in control."

"Be confident, but
never to cocky to learn.
Know when to hang
in there, and when it's
time to move on."

"Remember there is
power in the tongue.
Your words can be pleasant
or like a bee that has been stung.

Words spoken can
not be returned,
and like a bell
that has sounded
they can't be unrung."

"Don't be stubborn,
admit when you're wrong.
Apologize when necessary
and don't cling to anger for long."

You taught me principals,
morals, and how to act sensible.
To respect, and help my brother,
and not let greed corrupt me
from having compassion for others.

As a strong man you
taught me to lead
and to take a stand,
and never compromise
my identity or who I am!

Dad, thank you for
teaching me to
stand up… and
be a man!

(When Ryan finishes reading the poem "A Man" we see a black back drop that is lit up with the words "Dad You Are My Hero.")

Ryan: *(Ryan backs up to the backdrop, nods his head and rubs his hands together. Ryan then looks down at his watch)* It's getting late. I need to get home and get ready for my big day tomorrow. *He walks off the stage swiftly. We then see a man to the left in spotlight with dim lights who briefly plays the saxophone. The lights slowly fade down)*

II.

AWARDS
&
ACCOLADES

(Despite your awards and accolades never forget the love of family, and don't throw them shade. Always remember it was from your mother and father that you were made.)

The lights come up and we see Ryan and his wife who was playing the piano in the opening scene in their kitchen. They are sitting at the table drinking coffee and talking. His wife's name is Lisa.

Ryan: Hey Lisa, I'm so excited about the award ceremony tomorrow. It's such an honor to be receiving an award for my accomplishments in the field of science and medicine. Your man is smart!

Lisa: Honey you deserve it! You work so hard, and you've helped so many people. You have an extremely busy life, yet you make time for others. For example, the event you had yesterday at the theater honoring your parents was absolutely beautiful and selfless! You're also a great family man and you do such a good job with our four kids. You're God sent my husband, and I love you! Not only are you a magnificent husband and scientist, but you're also an awesome singer too! You stole my heart when you sang to me on our very first date.

Ryan: Sweetheart, you're the best! The song came from my heart. You have musical skills too and can play that piano! I was so amazed when I heard you play. You're super pretty and talented! We could make a dynamic musical team. Perhaps, when our kids are all grown, we can hit the road together. I love to sing, and you love to play the piano. It will be perfect!

Lisa: (*Chuckles and says*) The future is far away, and the kids are still small. Let's just focus on today and your big award ceremony tomorrow. I'm so proud of you. (*Lisa kisses her husband on the forehead and says*) Goodnight, I'm heading to bed, don't be up too late my dear. Tomorrow is a big day for you. (*Lisa exits off stage to the couple's bedroom*)

Ryan: Goodnight my beautiful wife. I'll join you in a bit. I want to practice saying my big speech that I wrote. I wouldn't want to mess up on such an important day. I'm so happy my family will be there to watch me receive my award. (*Says in a sad manner*) I just wish my little brother Calvin could be there too.

Lisa: *(Lisa comes back out from the bedroom and puts her arms around her husband in a caring manner)* Honey, don't think about Calvin right now. I know you get sad and down every time you think about him. It wasn't your fault. Tomorrow is your big day. Promise me you won't focus on Calvin right now.

Ryan: Honey I promise. I'm just going to practice my speech.

Lisa: *(She kisses her husband) Good night again Ryan. (Exits off stage back to the bedroom)*

Ryan: Goodnight. *(Ryan walks out of the kitchen into the living room. He is reciting his speech in the mirror. He then sits in a black recliner chair in the living room and continues to go over his speech. He looks side to side to make sure his wife is not around and then he looks up to the ceiling and says)* Calvin, man I miss and love you. Why did you have to let money and fame corrupt you? Why did you let the vultures and the knaves turn you against your own family? Why?

(Ryan lets the seat back in the recliner and lays his head back. He falls into a deep sleep and he keeps asking the question why. Ryan is having a flashback in his dream. He is calling his younger brother Calvin from their parents' home and is talking to him on the phone. It's their mother's birthday. The family is waiting on Calvin before they start the party)

Flashback/Ryan's Dream*:*

Ryan: *(Calls Calvin's house and is excited)* Hey Calvin did you forget it's mom's birthday? Where are you man? We're all waiting for you to get here before mom blows out her candles!

Calvin: No, I didn't forget, and I'm not coming to the party. I'm too busy, so let it go!

Ryan: What do you mean you're not coming?

Calvin: Just what I said. I'm not coming. I don't have time! I got more important things to do. You know the fans and the press are counting on me. I need to practice for my big golf tournament coming up next month. Tammy and I are heading out the house to the golf course right now. I need to get off this phone with you. I can't keep Tammy waiting. (*Tammy is Calvin's girlfriend. She is in the background calling Calvin's name)*

Tammy: Calvin come on let's go! We don't have all day. I need to get my hair and nails done after your practice and pick up a new outfit, including the shoes and purse. The shops close early today. I have to stay looking good you know! Who's that on the phone… your leeching family?

Ryan: Calvin why do you let that girl talk so bad about your family? You need to put her in check!

Calvin: I don't control her. She has a mouth and mind of her own. In my eyes, she can do no wrong. Don't bash Tammy. She's my woman and she is so fine!

Ryan: And disrespectful. *(Pause)* Calvin you know dad raised you to lead and to be a man! Why do you let that girl boss you around like a little puppy? You act like you don't know mom or dad no more. You don't visit, you don't call them. You missed Kendra's college graduation, and Rhonda's wedding. You let your sisters down. We are all waiting for you, so mom can blow out her candles.

Calvin: Look, I'm a grown man now! Anyway, you're the "good son." I don't have time for all that family stuff, besides Tammy and I are going to be starting our own family soon. Ryan, I told you I'm busy.

Ryan: You guys are not even married yet! Man, stop being a jerk! Mom sacrificed so much and gave you so much of her time. Your ego is really getting out of control. You need to check yourself. How in the hell can you be too busy for your own mama? In fact, mom was the one who signed you up for golf in the first place, or did you forget? She and dad purchased your very first set of golf clubs when you were eight years old and paid for all your golf lessons. Never forget your humble beginnings my little brother.

Don't let the awards, accolades, fame, and money go to your head. Dad always said money and too much success could corrupt a man. Don't let the screaming sounds and flattering comments from fans make you lose your common sense.

Mom is so sweet and caring. I can't stand how you just break her heart with no remorse. You're still young Calvin. You can make things right. Don't miss mom's birthday. She'll be happy to see you. Don't disappoint her.

Tammy: *(Says in an irritating manner as she walks in the room smacking on gum and rolling her eyes)* Why are you still on the phone with him? This is how you get a nerdy, overprotective, and bossy big brother off the phone. I swear your family is so lame! Let's go little puppy. *(Takes the phone out of Calvin's hand and hangs it up)*

Ryan: Calvin, Calvin! No you didn't just let her call you a little puppy and hang up in my face. Calvin, hello… hello… *(Ryan shakes his head in disgust and places his cell phone in his pocket)*

Calvin grabs his golf clubs. Calvin and Tammy walk out the house and get into a blue Mercedes-Benz. Just as Calvin is backing out of his driveway, his car is hit by a drunk driver, that doesn't stop. Tammy screams and then passes out. Calvin is hurt and covered in blood. He's still conscious, but weak because he is losing blood. He reaches for his cell phone and dials his mother's number.

Mother: *(The phone rings. She steps away from her party in the kitchen into the family room to answer the phone where it is quiet. She shuts the door between the kitchen and the living room so she doesn't hear the noise from her grandchildren playing and family talking. Everyone is at her house waiting to celebrate her birthday)* Hello.

Calvin: Hello Mama.

Mother: Calvin is that you? It's so nice to hear from you son. I can't wait to see you! Everyone is already here. (*Says in a concerning manner*) Are you ok? You don't sound so good.

Calvin: (*Moaning and in pain*) Mama, I just want to say I'm sorry. I lost my mind. The money, fame, and Tammy corrupted me. I should have honored you. I just want you to know, I never stopped loving you. Tell dad I said thank you for teaching me to be a man. He did his job as a father. I failed as a son. I wasn't wise enough to listen to him. I got so big-headed and arrogant, that I thought I did everything on my own. I started listening to the wrong people who really didn't have my best interest in heart. You and dad did so much for me. I was an ungrateful son. Please forgive me. I'm just so happy, I got a chance to hear your voice. Happy Birthday Mama... I can't hold on any longer. (*Calvin drops his cell phone, and slumps over the steering wheel*)

Mother: (*Screaming and crying*) Calvin what do you mean you can't hold on any longer? Calvin don't go, Calvin please don't go! (*She drops the phone and starts crying*)

Father: *(Ryan's father is in the kitchen with the rest of the family waiting for his wife to return from the phone. He is looking around side to side)* Where is your mother? I know she is stalling around waiting on Calvin. I hope he shows up.

Tasha: Dad you know Calvin is not coming. He hasn't been the same person since he met Tammy. Lately, all he seems to care about is Tammy and making money playing golf. He's been throwing shade at the family since he's been winning all those awards and accolades in golf. He missed mama's birthday last year. I know she was sad that he didn't show up. You know Calvin is "Mr. I'm so Important."

Rhonda: Tasha be nice. Besides Calvin is his own man. You can't blame others for his actions. If he wants to come, he will come.

Father: Rhonda's right! Somethings you can't blame on others, you have to make your own decisions in life. As a man you must know when to lead. You can't go blaming Tammy. It's up to Calvin to do the right thing and show up to his mama's birthday.

Kendra: I'm sorry, I have to agree with Tasha. Every since Calvin got with Tammy he's been acting differently. He didn't even show up at my college graduation. Who misses their little sister's graduation? And somebody please tell me when was the last time Calvin has called this house. Mama and daddy's number has been the same for over twenty years.

Also, when I went over to Calvin's house the other day, I didn't see any of our family photos that used to be on his fireplace mantle. When I asked Calvin about the photos he said, "Tammy is moving things around and redecorating." She just moved into his place a week ago and has already changed his whole entire house around. I'm telling you he is not the same! Tammy has Calvin wrapped around her little finger. He's whipped! Plus, like Tasha said, he's been winning all those golf tournaments and it's gone straight to his head! People run around worshiping him like he's Jesus Christ. He acts like he doesn't even know his own family. He's so damn arrogant!

Rhonda: Ladies stop all the bickering. If you believe Calvin has any shortcomings pray for him. Besides, it's mom's birthday. It's her special day! Let's focus on her right now and not Calvin. Let us be happy and appreciate those who are here to celebrate mom. Ok ladies on the count of three rub your nails together and say, "Family Peace." 1,2,3...

All of Ryan's Sisters: (*Each of them takes their own hands and rub their nails together and say*) "Family Peace!" *This is a ritual they made up when they were little girls. If any of them started fussing about who won in jacks, jump rope, chores or anything that would cause confusion, they agreed to keep the peace by rubbing their nails together. They were older but they still did this sisterly ritual to prevent family arguments with each other. The sisters stop arguing and begin talking about other things.*

Johnathon: Daddy where's grandma? I want cake.

Ryan: I think your grandma is in the living room on the phone. I'll go get her, and don't you touch that cake.

Johnathon: Ok daddy.

Ryan: *(Ryan walks out of the kitchen into the living room to get this mom)* Mom where are you? *(He notices his mom is crying)* Mom why are you crying?

Mother: *(She continues to cry and passes the phone to Ryan)* Here take the phone Ryan, it's your brother Calvin. *(She walks into her bedroom and lies down. She is overcome by grief)*

Ryan: *(Ryan takes the phone)* Calvin so you had a change of heart? Mom's so happy that you're coming she's crying. Hurry up and get here. I was just coming to get mom so we could start her party. You know how she likes to wait until all her children arrive before she blows the candles out and cuts the cake. Calvin…

Tammy: *(Tammy is now conscious and has picked up Calvin's cell phone from the seat of the car. She is screaming, and a little disoriented)* This is not Calvin! This is Tammy. Who is this?

Ryan: Tammy it's Ryan, what's wrong?

Tammy: (*Sobbing and angry*) I'll tell you what's wrong. You killed your brother. The ambulance just took Calvin away. We were trying to leave the house and get to the golf course, but you kept trying to convince him to come to some stupid birthday party for your mom. If we would've just left a second earlier Calvin might still be alive. We were hit by a drunk driver when Calvin was backing the car out of the driveway. You killed him Ryan. It's all your fault! You killed him! (*Tammy continues to cry*)

Ryan: (*Drops the phone, and starts shouting why... why... why...?*

It is now morning time. Ryan fell asleep on the black recliner chair with his folded speech in his hand and is still dreaming about his brother. His children are awakened by his shouting. His four children enter into the living room rubbing their eyes. Ryan has two daughters and two sons. Nita his youngest daughter is 4, Rebeca is 7, Johnathon is 5, and Davis is 11. His daughter Nita and his son Johnathon jump on his lap and wake him up)

Nita: Daddy why do you keep shouting why, why, why? You woke me up!

All the other Kids: Yeah dad, you woke us all up.

Davis: Dad are you ok? Looks like you were having a bad dream.

Ryan: Kids, I'm okay. It was just a dream. *(Taken back by the daylight)* Is it morning already? *(Ryan gets out of the recliner chair and walks over to the window. He pulls the curtains back slightly, peeks outside and is greeted by the bright morning sun shining in his eye)*

Rebeca: *(Concerned)* Dad were you dreaming about Uncle Calvin again?

Ryan: Sweetie I'm ok. *(Ryan is obviously shaken by his dream. He often has flashbacks and dreams about Calvin's car accident. He tries to act like he's ok so his children don't worry about him)*

Ryan's Children: *(All the children are now standing around their dad and looking sleepy)*

Lisa: *(Lisa enters the family room where Ryan and the children are. She is wearing her housecoat and slippers)* Honey you fell asleep on the couch. I didn't even notice that you weren't in bed until I woke up this morning. I was so tired; I slept the whole night through. Hey you kids! Go get dressed. Today is an incredibly special day. Your very smart dad is getting an award!

Davis: *(Sleepy and irritated)* Mom it's 7a.m. in the morning! The award ceremony is not until 1pm. Why do we have to get dressed so early? I'm trying to go back to bed and get some more sleep.

Lisa: *(Lisa is worried about getting to the award ceremony on time)* Boy don't you go back to sleep right now! Besides getting dressed, you have to eat breakfast, and you never know about the traffic. Once we get there we also have to find parking…

Ryan: *(Interrupts his wife while she is talking to their son Davis)* Lisa you don't have to explain. *(Says in a stern manner to his son)* You don't run things around here Davis. Don't back talk your mother. We're the parents and you're the child, now go get dressed like your mom said.

Davis: Yes sir. (*Davis, his brother and all his sisters run off to their rooms to get dressed*)

Ryan and his wife Lisa are in the living room talking.

Rebecca: (*Runs back into the living room and is excited. She has a silver sparkling dress in her hand*) Mom can me and Nita wear our special sparkling dress? Please! Can we mama, please?

Lisa: Sure baby.

Rebecca: (*With excitement*) Yes! (*She runs back into her room jumping up and down and tells her little sister Nita*) Mom said yes!

Nita: Yay!

Lisa: (*Talking to Ryan*) I guess we need to go get dressed too.

Ryan: This is true!

Ryan and Lisa both enter into their room to get dressed. Everyone comes out of their rooms and is dressed nicely. Ryan, his wife, and all of their children exits out the front door of the house. The lights fade and then picks up at the award ceremony. They all arrive at the award ceremony and are seated at a table upfront. Ryan's mom, dad, and three sisters are also seated at the table. Ryan is speaking at the podium.

Ryan: I want to thank God, my wife, mother, father and my sisters for their love and support. (*He raises his award up in the air and says*) This is also for you Calvin. You will always be my little brother.

The lights fade after Ryan gives his speech. We hear the saxophone playing. Ryan, his wife and four kids return back home from the award ceremony. The children all ran to their rooms. Lisa and Ryan are in the living room talking about the award ceremony. They are both sitting on the couch together and enjoying each other's company and conversation.

Lisa: Let me go check on the kids Ryan. *(She looks into all the kids' rooms and then returns to the living room)* The kids are all sound to sleep.

Ryan: Well, it's time to pour the wine! Baby it's party time! *(Ryan does a funny little dance and goes into the kitchen and returns back with two wine glasses and a bottle of wine)* Here's to a beautiful wife! Let's toast to us. May our love last forevermore!

Ryan and Lisa: *(Raise and tap their wine glasses together)* Cheers!

Ryan: *(Ryan walks over to his desk which is in the living room and pulls out a piece of paper from his top desk draw)* Lisa I've been working on this poem, and I want to dedicate it to you. Do you want to hear it?

Lisa: Of course I do! I'm so flattered Ryan.

Ryan: Sweetheart this is for you *(Ryan begins to read the poem "Forevermore")*

<u>Forevermore</u>

If there was
a recipe for
a perfect wife
you will be it.

You were the
missing puzzle in
in my life,
the perfect fit.

You're much more
than good looks,
and you have more
knowledge than
a thousand books.

You remind me
of a delicious cake,
and I love being
next to you each
morning I awake.

You're precious,
one of a kind,
and to this very day
you blow my mind.

I feel grateful,
and truly blessed.
Your love is special
I must confess.

I give to you
my heart and time,
because a love like
yours, I'll never find.

When you were made
they broke the mold,
you're the best I've
ever had, truth be told.

You mean the world to me,
bringing sunshine and glee!
There is no other
place I rather be.

You're no secret
everybody knows
how I feel about
you wherever we go!

You can find comfort
within my arms.
Together we enjoy life and
weather through the storms.

You're beautiful the
love of my life
and it makes me so
proud to call you my wife.

You can count
on me for sure,
and my love
forevermore!

Lisa: Ryan that is so beautiful! What a beautiful poem. You're going to make me start crying.

Ryan: It's just a little something, something. Lisa marrying you was one of the best decisions I've ever made. God sent you to me and I wasn't going to be foolish and let you get away. I knew you were a good thing the time I laid eyes on you. Not only are you a great wife, but you're also a terrific mother to our children, and I love and appreciate you.

Lisa: Ryan, you make me feel so special and cherished. I never have to question or doubt your love for me. I appreciate and love you too. I still remember one of our romantic dates on the beach, and I wrote a poem about it. I took the poem and made it into a song, and I want to sing it to you right now. (*Lisa walks over to the piano and starts to play and sing the song "Our Love Poem"*)

Our Love Poem

I watched the sun go up
and then I watched
the sun go down.
Moon is shining brightly
like a crystal ball.
Stars are shining brightly
against the black-purple sky,
wind is blowing gently
It's a cool dark night.

Waters calling out to us
looking clean and clear,
and you're whispering
something sweet into my ear.
You embrace my body,
and we lie in the sand,
making love together
on this paradise land.

And it's you that I want baby,
it's you that I need darling.
You that I want baby,
it's you that I need.
Forever yours, forever more.
Together forever,
This is our love poem.

Lisa: Ryan that was such a special memory for me. The beach was extremely beautiful that night and I felt so happy in your arms. You know after all these years you still make my heartbeat. I'm a sucker for that big smile of yours!

Ryan: You make my heart beat too, but we need to carry this party over into the next room. I like your poetry, piano playing, and singing but you know what I like even more…

Lisa: Yes I do, I surely do…

Ryan: Girl, I always said you was smart! (*Ryan picks his wife up off the couch and proceeds to carry her into their bedroom. He then sings a few bars of some romantic songs as he gazes deeply into Lisa eyes*)

Lisa: (*Lisa is smiling from ear to ear and closes the bedroom door when her husband passes through the doorway carrying her*)

The lights fade and we hear the saxophone playing. A new scene picks up with Tammy on her knees praying to God.

Tammy: Dear God, I miss Calvin so much. (*She looks down and rubs her pregnant stomach and begins to cry*) My baby will never know his father. We had already picked out his name, Calvin Jr. My sweetheart was so happy and proud that he was having a boy. We had the room all decorated. God I'm so sorry. I was jealous of the relationship that Calvin had with his family. I was especially jealous of his mom. I wanted to take him from his family. I wanted him to only love me and our new son. We were to be his new family, and in my mind his only family. I was dealt the hand I played. Karma, revenge, and payback knocked on my door with no sympathy. My Calvin was taken from me and our son to be. My heart hurts so bad, and now I know how it feels when I took Calvin away from his family. The heavy and ugly stone I rolled up the hill came rolling back on me. The chickens had come home to roost. Please forgive me God and take away this pain. I guess I'll go take my bath now. I have enough tears to fill up the whole tub. Oh, this hurts so bad. (*Tammy gets up from the ground and wipes her tears. She exits off stage and we hear bath water running. Tammy is in the bathroom taking a warm bubble bath to calm* *her nerves and is singing the song "God please take this pain away")*

The lights fade and we hear the saxophone playing. A new scene picks up with Tammy calling Ryan's sister Tasha. She walks over to the phone, picks it up and dials Tasha's number.

Tammy: *(Calls Tasha on the phone)* Tasha I need to tell you something.

Tasha: *(She is not thrilled to hear from Tammy)* What is it Tammy?

Tammy: I'm pregnant with Calvin's son.

Tasha: *(Surprised)* Really!

Tammy: Yes, and please forgive me for being so evil. I was so jealous of the close and strong relationship Calvin had with his family. Tasha your family is so awesome. Your parents are so great. I feel so ashamed. I was jealous because I never had a good relationship with my parents. My father and mother divorced when I was ten years old. We moved away to another state, so I never spent much time with my dad.

My mother and I were never close. We argued all the time. Plus, growing up as a bi-racial child, I often felt confused and left out. When I met Calvin he was like an Angel. He was the only person who showed me kindness, security, and the love I so desperately craved for.

I know Calvin always loved his family. He got really upset at me when I moved his family portraits from the mantle.

I remember it clear as day (*Tammy flashes back to a scene of her and Calvin*)

Flashback:

I came home from shopping. I bought some new things to decorate the house and for the baby's new room. Calvin wasn't home yet. I was so excited about all the new things I had purchased. I called my mom on the phone to tell her what I bought for the baby and the house, but she didn't pick up. I got upset and left her a bitter and angry message. She's never around when I need someone to talk to. I hung up the phone and I thought to myself, I wish I had a mom like Calvin's mom. As I was thinking out loud, I turned around and saw all the pictures Calvin had on the mantel of his family. I especially got angry when I saw the picture of his mom holding him when he was a baby in a frame that said, "Love Always for My Mom." He also had pictures of him and his dad and a bunch of other family photos. He had a picture with you, Rebecca, Kendra, Ryan, your mom, and dad all smiling together at a park in front of a tree. The picture frame had the words "My Family" on it. I just wept hot tears and became angry and envious. I wanted a family like Calvin's so bad! In a fit of anger and jealousy, I ran into the kitchen and grabbed a grocery bag from under the cabinet and threw all of the pictures in it. I wanted pictures of me and Calvin in the house and nobody else. Just when I was coming back in the house from throwing the pictures in the garbage can outside, Calvin walked in.

Calvin: (*Walking through the front door happily with his golf clubs. He's humming and singing*) Hey Tammy I'm home! (*Calvin looks around for Tammy who is coming in from the back yard. He then looks at the mantel and notices that his pictures are not there. He screams Tammy's name louder and is now upset*) Tammy! Where are my family photos?

Tammy (*Nervously comes running in the house*) Babe there right in the back yard on the table. I'll go get them. (*Tammy runs in the backyard quickly and takes the bag with the pictures out of the trash can. She runs back into the house and shows Calvin the bag. She pulls the pictures out one by one and shows them to Calvin. Tammy puts the photos back in the bag and places the bag on the sofa*)

Calvin (*Irritated*) Tammy why were my pictures in the backyard?

Tammy: I was dusting off the fireplace mantel and I didn't want the pictures to fall in the frame and break. I decided to take a little time out from decorating and cleaning, so I went in the backyard to enjoy the sunshine, read my book, and dip my feet in the pool. I accidentally took the photos with me. I noticed they were in my hand when I got in the back yard, so I just put them on the patio table next to me. I forgot to bring them back in. Why are you so upset with me little puppy? It was just a minor incident of forgetfulness. I'll make sure to put them back when I'm done decorating. (*She takes Calvin's hands and* *wraps them around her pregnant waist and gives him a great big kiss*)

Calvin: (*He is calming down and is also kissing her*) I'm sorry Tammy. You know those pictures mean the world to me. Especially the photo of my mom holding me in the hospital when I was first born.

Tammy*: (Starts to sniffle, and is seeking sympathy)* I know honey, that's why I wanted to dust off the mantel and clean the glass on the picture frames so they could look nice and shiny for you.

Calvin: It's ok Tammy about the pictures, I know you were only trying to do something nice. Please forgive me for being angry.

Tammy: It's ok babe. (*When Calvin turns she has a sly smile on her face and quietly giggles. She mumbles softly under her breath*) He will believe anything I tell him. Anything.

Calvin: (*Turns to walk upstairs to the bedroom*) Well I'm heading to take a nap. I got up super early to hit golf balls this morning and I'm starting to really feel beat.

Talk to you later babe. *(Calvin walks in his room yawning and goes to sleep)*

Tammy: *(Tammy had got so caught up in her flashback of Calvin and the photos that she almost forgot that she was talking to Tasha on the phone)* Tasha are you still there?

Tasha: *(Concerned and compassionate)* Yes I'm still here. Tammy slow down and take a breath. Don't upset yourself. You just said you were pregnant. It's a bad memory, a flashback. Let go of it and let it be the past.

Tammy: *(Crying)* Tasha I'm so sorry about trying to get rid of the photos. I only wanted Calvin to love and care for me. Since I'm cleansing my soul, I have something else to admit.

Tasha: Ok I'm listening.

Tammy: I used to delete phone messages when your mom called so Calvin couldn't hear them. She always left him nice and sweet messages. *(Sadly)* I wish my mom would leave me nice messages like the ones Calvin would get from his mom, but she never did.

I even answered some of Calvin texts messages from your mom pretending like I was him. The messages would always end with "I love you," but I always made sure not to text back "I love you too." Some of my responses to your mom were mean. One night Calvin and I were getting ready for bed and his mom called. Calvin was in the shower and the phone was on the nightstand. I picked up his phone and turned it off. I even blocked your mom's phone number on a few occasions. I thought I could cause confusion and division between the two of them, but your mom didn't fall for it. She's like a mother bear. She is so caring, motherly, and compassionate. I don't ever recall my mom telling me "I love you", oh how I long to hear those three letter words from her. I was so jealous, selfish, and insecure. I feel so guilty, and I've asked God for forgiveness.

Tasha since I am carrying Calvin's son, I will always be a part of your family. Please forgive me. I also want to apologize to your parents and the rest of your family. I hope they will forgive me too.

Tasha: What made you call me?

Tammy: Tasha since we're both about the same age I felt comfortable enough to call you. I felt so bad, I had to talk to someone, and get this off my chest. I really don't have any friends or family to talk to. I hope you're ok with me calling you.

Tasha: It's cool Tammy. No worries. I'm fine with you calling me. We all make mistakes. I'm not perfect, in fact, nobody is. I'm glad you recognized that you were wrong and was brave enough to apologize. Some people are pig-headed and will never recognize when they're wrong or apologize. I forgive you, and I'm quite sure the rest of my family will too.

Tammy: Thank you Tasha for understanding and listening, this means so much to me.

Tasha: Hey, it's my parents' 35th anniversary this weekend, why don't you come and make peace with the family? I'm quite sure everyone will be excited to know about the baby.

Tammy: Thanks for the invite Tasha. I will be there!

III.
CELEBRATING

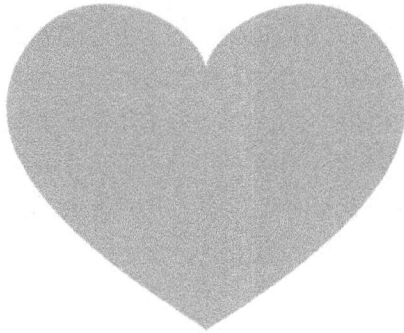

(Celebrate family, for family is a special gift. Hold them close to your heart, be grateful, forgiving, and uplift.)

The lights fade and we hear the saxophone playing. A new scene picks up at Ryan's parents' home. Everyone is there celebrating his parents' 35th anniversary, including his mom's best friend of 50 years. Everything is decorated in blue and lavender, her favorite colors. In the center of the table is a big heart cake with the words "Happy Anniversary." The heart is her favorite shape because it represents love. She has on her favorite lavender blouse, a blue topaz heart necklace, and is wearing a beautiful tanzanite ring (an anniversary gift from her husband) that's shimmering shades of blue, purple, and lavender.

Mother: Everything looks beautiful! Thanks for coming to our 35th Anniversary party, and a special thanks to Ryan for coordinating everything. Ryan you're such a good son. I know it's me and your dad's anniversary, (*Looks at her husband and smiles*) Your dad knows how much I love him, but I want to read this poem for you.

Ryan: Mom this day is about you and dad, not me.

Mother: Ryan you're a part of us. You remind me so much of your dad. Wise, strong, caring and a good family man. (*She reads the poem "A Good Son"*)

A GOOD SON

A good son
wants to see
you happy, and
never sad and blue.

He will always
be there for you.
He shows gratitude
and appreciates
the things you do!

Your sacrifices, dedication,
and hard work you did for him,
he will never forget!
He will not cause you
undue sorrow or
have you regret.

A good son will
show you honor
and make you
feel really proud.

He will never badmouth
or disrespect you, in person
or in front of a crowd.

He will check
on you to make
sure you're okay, and
will cherish and love you
until your dying day.

My son you are wise,
noble and strong,
and you know the
difference between
right and wrong.

You lead, and
you don't allow
others to deter
your path.
You have dignity,
character, honor,
and class!

A good son is
what you are.
You will
always be special,
and loved.
Keep shining like a star!

Ryan: Mom that was absolutely beautiful!

Mother: Ryan you are my first born, and you have brought so much joy over the years. You helped me so much with your younger sisters and brother. You and all of my children are my heart, a blessing to a mother's soul. Children are a treasure, a gift from God.

Kendra: All except for one child mama. There's always a black sheep in the family. There's always that one!

Mother: Hush your mouth Kendra. I won't allow negativity at my anniversary party.

Kendra: Mom no disrespect, but everybody knows Calvin is an ingrate. He's so self-centered and arrogant. What kind of son speaks ill-will of his parents who did so much for him? I'll tell you, an ungrateful son! Do you have a poem called, An Ungrateful Son?

Mother: (*Sternly*) Kendra, I said hush. I don't want to hear it, not today. We don't sow discord in this house. Today is a happy day. A day of love and celebration! Besides, I raised you all to be close and to help each other. There are too many battles to fight in this world, you don't need to fight amongst each other. Our family bond will not be broken! In this family we uplift and pray to God for any

shortcomings that we may have. Family is to be cherished and not taken for granted.
None of us knows our last days here on earth.

Kendra: Yes mother. (*Kendra realizes she is upsetting her mom, so she reaches out to hug her*) You're right mom, today is about love and celebration. You and dad are awesome, and it makes me so proud to call you my parents. I will always love and be grateful to you both. (*Joking, and with a big smile*) Mom that was a nice poem about a son, but what about a daughter?

Mother: No worries my sweet daughters. I have a poem for you girls too. I wrote it for this special event. I want to dedicate this poem to all three of my lovely daughters.

Father: (*Talking to his wife jokingly*) Honey you're always looking out for those kids. Kids who are now full grown. It's our anniversary celebration, why are you writing poems about them?

Mother: (*Talking to her husband with a big smile as she proudly confesses her love for her children*) Honey, a mother's love never stops no matter their age. They will always be my babies! Girls this poem is for you! (*She reads the poem "My Lovely Daughter"*

MY LOVELY DAUGHTER

My lovely daughter
you are a gift from God,
and in my life you
are a blissful part.

You're respectful,
caring and you
have a good heart.

You're precious in
so many ways,
and you're radiant like
the sun on a perfect day!

You're great company,
and you visit and phone.
I'm blessed you
didn't break my heart
or leave me all alone.

You show your
appreciation in
so many ways,
and there's so
many good things
about you that
I could say!

I love you
my daughter
more than you
would ever know.

You're beautiful, wise
and you make
my heart glow!

You give unselfishly
to help others,
and I'm so happy
and proud to
be your mother.

Kendra, **Tasha,** and **Rhonda**: Aw… mom that was so sweet!

Rhonda: Mom you have such a good heart. I agree with dad. It's you guys 35th Anniversary, no more talking about us children. (*Smiles and places her hands on her mom's shoulder*) Your grown children.

Mother: *(Smiles)* You're right Rhonda.

Davis: Grandma I wrote a poem for you and grandad. (*Davis looks at his Aunt Rhonda for approval*) Auntie Rhonda, this poem is about grandma and grandpa.

Rhonda: Davis as long as the poem is for your grandma and grandpa, you're good to go! It's their anniversary.

Davis: Ok

Rebecca: *(Excited)* I helped too!

Davis: True little sister you did help… some, but since I'm the oldest grandchild I get to read it.

Rebecca: *(Reluctantly)* Ok.

Davis: Grandma and grandpa, this is for you. *(Davis reads the poem "A Grandparents Love")*

A Grandparents Love

Grandparents are fun
and they love you like
flowers do the sun.

They spoil you
and let you do
just about anything.
Grandparents love you
so much and like a bird
their hearts sings.

Cookies, cake, candy
whatever they can
give is yours,
and you're so happy
when you walk through
your grandparents' doors!

No chores at grandparents
house, but you offer to help
out of love, and it's what
your parents taught you to do,
but grandparents say "sit down
there's no chores here for you!"

Fishing, shopping, parks, cooking
they want to spend time with you.
Grandparents brag about your
accomplishments and they
constantly dote on you.

Grandparents are wise
and tell you stories
about things that
happened long ago,
interesting facts that
hunger your mind to know.

They tell you funny stories
about your parents when
they were little, it makes
you laugh so hard.
Grandparents are an
ace, a very powerful card.

They're like your
parents, but more like
icing on the cake.
The love and
bond we have for
them is something that
will never break.

Ryan: (*Looks at his mom*) What funny stories have you told Davis about me mom?

Mother: (*Chuckles*) It's a grandma and grandkid's secret. Anyhow Davis and Rebecca that was a beautiful poem!

Father: Yes my little grands that was a very nice poem. I'm loving all the poetry being shared today. Davis you and your sister did a wonderful job!

Davis and Rebeca: Thanks!

Mother: You little rascals come give grandma and grandpa a big hug.

Davis and Rebeca (*Run and give their grandparents a great big hug*)

Kendra (*In a joking manner*) Does anybody else have a poem? I'm like little Johnny (*Looks over at her youngest nephew who is 5 years old*) I'm ready for some cake too.

Courtney: Auntie Kendra, we didn't write a poem but me and Kelly made up a dance routine for grandma and grandpa.

Johnny: (*Grabs his face and says*) Oh brother, can we just eat the cake now! Grandma and Grandpa can you watch their dance later?

Lisa: Johnny be patient.

Johnny: (*Eyeing at the cake*) Yes mama.

Mother: Johnny come sit on grandma's lap and I promise I'll let you be the first person to get a piece of cake after your grandpa and me.

Johnny: (*Runs happily to sit on his grandma's lap*) Ok grandma.

Ryan: Mama, don't spoil him.

Kendra: Courtney, your grandparents would love to see you girls dance.

Courtney & Kelly: Ok this is for your 35th Anniversary grandma and grandpa.
(*Courtney and Kelly perform a hip-hop dance routine they made up*)

Everybody claps for the girls when they finish their dance routine.

Courtney & Kelly: We love you grandma and grandpa! *(They both bow and take a seat)*

Kendra: *(Sarcastically)* Is there anybody else who wants to sing, dance, or say a poem?

Edith: *(Clears her throat)* Um… that will be me. Your mom and I have known each other for 50 plus years. We've been best friends since elementary school and roommates in college. I was the maid of honor at her wedding. Our friendship is special. I want to dedicate this poem to my beautiful and best friend Julie. *(Edith reads the poem a "Friend Is")*

A FRIEND IS

A friend is someone
you can count on,
in good and bad times.
A friend will be
there to help you,
when you feel you're
losing your mind.

A friend is someone
who genuinely cares.
They're not stingy
or selfish, and
will gladly share.

They care about your
happiness and are delighted
when you achieve.
A friend is never jealous
when you prosper or succeed!
They will be in
your corner cheering
for you indeed!

Someone you can
have fun with
and to share
a good laugh.

They don't try
to dictate your
every move or
control your path.

They will tell you
the truth, but only
out of love,
and will stick
with you tight
like a hand in glove.

It's not about
your clothes, car,
house, or money.
You don't need to
showboat, impress,
or act phony.

With a real friend,
you can relax
and be yourself.
No need to put
on airs, pretending
to be someone else.

They love you
if you have a
little, or a lot.

Their friendship isn't
based on titles, looks,
or what you got!

A friend is someone
you should never
take advantage of
and some are closer
than your own
relatives or blood.

My buddy,
my homie
this poem is
dedicated to you.
I'm lucky to have
a friend who is
loyal, kind, and true!

Mother: Thank you Edith. I really enjoyed that poem. Girl ditto everything you said. You're my homie to the end!

Rebecca: Grandma what's a homie?

Mother: A homie means a good friend.

Rebecca: Grandma, we call it BFF. BFF stands for best friend forever.

Mother: *(Looking at Rebecca smiling)* Ok baby! BFF is good too.

Johnathon: *(Exasperated)* Grandma, can we please eat the cake! Please…

Mother: Johnathon let's check with your dad and Auntie Kendra they're hosting this lovely celebration.

Ryan: *(Looking at Kendra)* Johnathon looks like your auntie Kendra is doing a great job hosting. Be patient we will get to the cake soon enough.

Kendra: Everybody has said a poem or dedicated something to our very lovely couple. Mom and dad are you ready to cut your cake?

Father: I always let your mom do the honor of cutting the cake first. Ladies first. *(Looks at his wife)* Baby are you ready?

Mother: *(Looks at the cake admiring it. There is a big candle on the cake with the number 35 on it)* I sure am! Let's blow out the candle together first.

Mother and Father: *(They blow out the candle, kiss each other, and say)* I love you!

Mother: *(Picks up knife to cut the cake)* Finally, Johnathon grandma is going to cut the cake. *(Just when she reaches to cut the cake the doorbell rings and she puts the knife back down on the table)* Who can that be?

Kendra: *(Running to the door)* I'll get it mom. *Kendra opens the front door and to her surprise in walks pregnant Tammy. Kendra's mouth is wide open with surprise.* Tammy what are you doing here?

Tammy: Tasha invited me.

Kendra: *(Looking at her sister Tasha and then back at Tammy)* She did? *(Sarcastically)* Well how can we help you?

Tammy: Tasha invited me and I wanted to come wish your parents a happy 35th anniversary.

Tasha: Yes, Kendra I invited her.

Kendra: *(Looking at Tammy's stomach)* You sure didn't mess around. It's been less than a year and you're already pregnant by someone else.

Tammy: It's not what you think Kendra.

Kendra: *(In disbelief and annoyed)* Really!

Tasha: Kendra let Tammy explain.

Tammy: First of all, I want to apologize to Mr. and Mrs. Daniels for all the times I was rude and disrespectful. You're Calvin's parents and my elders. I should have shown you both more respect. I wanted all of Calvin's attention and to be the queen bee.

In fact, I want to apologize to your entire family for my nasty attitude. I admit I was jealous of your family tight and loving relationship.

Ryan I'm very sorry for blaming Calvin's accident on you. The truth of the matter is, I was rushing him out of the house so we would have time to get my nails, hair done and an outfit before the stores closed. If it was anybody's fault it was mine.

Please forgive me everyone. I want to make peace with the family.

Tasha: Tammy it's nobody's fault but the drunk driver who hit Calvin's car. Don't blame yourself.

Tammy: You're right Tasha.

Tasha: *(Smiling)* Hey guys, Tammy has some good news to share with everyone.

Tammy: *(With excitement)* I'm pregnant with Calvin's child. It's a boy! My Calvin Jr. I couldn't keep it a secret any longer. Besides as big as my stomach was getting, my secret was sure to be exposed. I was only one month pregnant at the time of the car accident so I wasn't showing.

Mother: *(Overwhelmed with joy)* Oh sweet Jesus! The blessings of children, a memory of my dear son Calvin.

Tammy: *(Grabs her side)* Oh no! I think the baby is coming now!

Johnathon: Can the baby wait until we eat cake? I think I'll be a hundred years old before I will ever get a piece of that cake.

Everybody: *(Laughing)*

Kendra: *(Laughing and shaking her head)* Sorry little John John babies don't wait.

Johnathon: *(Sad about the cake)* aw man!

The lights fade and we hear the saxophone playing. The scene picks up and everybody is at the hospital Tammy delivers a healthy 8 pound and nine ounce baby boy. Ryan's mom invites her to come stay at the house so Tammy and the baby are not alone.

Mother: Tammy come to the house and stay for at least two weeks. Kendra and I will help you with the baby.

Kendra: *(Shocked and taken back)* Mom, you know I'm looking to move any day. I love babies, but…

Mother: But nothing Kendra. Promise you will help.

Kendra: Let me think about it mom.

Father: *(Talking to his daughter)* Kendra you are the baby of the family. I think your mom is afraid of having an empty nest.

Mother: Not so… well maybe. I admit I miss the kids when they were small and I do want Kendra to stay a little while longer.

Kendra: Mom I need to spread my wings. I promise to visit. I can help Tammy when I visit.

Mother: Tammy when you get out of the hospital you come right over to the house. You're always welcome sweetheart, you and the baby.

Tammy: Thank you so much Mrs. Daniels for the invitation, we will be there.

Mother: Great! Besides my beautiful flowers and my family, I get so excited about little babies, especially my grandbabies. Kendra please stay just a little bit longer.

Kendra: Sure mom I'll stay and help. I'm a sucker for little babies too.

The scene fades.

The scene opens up in Ryan's living room and he is writing in a journal sitting at his desk. It is early in the morning and everyone in the house is asleep. Ryan is sipping on his coffee and making an entry in his personal journal.

Ryan writes and narrates:

Tammy and the baby came and stayed with my parents. Everything is going great. Tammy and the baby stayed longer than expected and Kendra is still looking for a place to move.

Mama received a call from the hospital. The Dr. told her Calvin is no longer in a coma. Everyone pretty much had given up on Calvin except mama. She told all of us she was going in for a routine checkup, but she was really going to pick up Calvin from the hospital. She didn't tell anyone because she wanted it to be a surprise. The doctor told her that Calvin awoke from his coma and was doing well enough to go home. He had been out of his coma for about two weeks and his memory was fully back. Mama called all of us over to the house. She said she had a big surprise! Everybody was surprised and shocked when we saw Calvin sitting on the living room couch. Tammy almost fainted. Calvin was so excited about his new son.

Calvin and Tammy worked out their differences. Calvin explained to Tammy that he had love for both her and mom and she need not get jealous. Calvin told Tammy, "God said leave your house and be with your wife, but he also said to honor your mother and father." Tammy apologized and reassured Calvin that she had made peace with his family. Tammy told Calvin she resented being so disrespectful to his family.

Calvin was happy that there was peace between Tammy and the family. He also told Tammy that she needed to personally make amends with her own mom as well, and she did.

Calvin proposed to Tammy and they got married. It was a beautiful wedding and everybody was there. Tammy's mom and even her dad who she hadn't seen in years showed up. The wedding was a beautiful celebration. I was the best man and Lisa was the maid of honor. All my sisters were bride maids. My sisters took in their sisters-in-law just like they were blood sisters. The women often got together for lunches, shopping, and girl getaways. Tammy finally had the sisters she always wanted.

Later in the year it was mom's birthday. Calvin was so excited. He planned and paid for all the decorations, food, and cake. We all tried to pitch in, but Calvin refused to accept any money from us and he wanted to plan everything! The hall was decorated in light blue and lavender, mom's favorite colors. Calvin vowed to never miss another one of mom's birthdays and he didn't.

We all had a great time at her party. It was another wonderful family celebration. Mom got so many gifts. We gave her flowers, candy, perfume, and her favorite store gift cards. We all pitched in and bought her a gold ring. On the inside of the ring it was engraved with "We Love You Mom." In the center of the ring was a flower that had hearts with the color of our birthstones surrounding it, and our names inscribed on it. Mom was so excited about the ring because it had all five of her children's names and their birthstones. Calvin knows how much mom loves live theater, and he bought her tickets for all of her favorite shows. We all had such a wonderful time, and mom was overjoyed!

I was so glad to see that my little brother Calvin had been enlightened. He was starting to become a man and he realized the importance and bond of family. He made peace with mama and the entire family. He apologized to Kendra for missing her college graduation. He even gave Kendra a card with a nice big check in it! Kendra used the money to help get herself a nice condo off the beach. She was so excited to finally be moving out of mom and dad's house.

Kendra did keep her promise to visit and so did all of us.

We also got together once a year for our big family picnic. Rhonda the oldest of my sisters made the best fried chicken. It was always perfectly seasoned and crispy. Tasha made the best potato salad, and Kendra the yummiest macaroni and cheese. I made the sweet yams. Everybody wanted the recipe for it, but I promised mom that I would only past the recipe down to my children. Calvin was the person who did all the grilling. He made the best barbecue ribs and his wife made both jambalaya, and gumbo, oh yeah! Mom and all the grandkids made the desserts. Dad was the salad king, and my wife Lisa always provided all the beverages, paper goods and utensils. We had so much fun playing games, telling jokes, eating, and just bonding as a family. I always looked forward to our big annual picnic.

Ryan: (*Finishes writing in his journal and places it in his desk draw*) Let me put this away for now.

Lisa: *(Enters living room where Ryan is and is tying her robe)* Honey you up early again writing in your journal?

Ryan: Yelp.

Lisa: Do you want some breakfast?

Ryan: Sure babe that will be great.

Scene fades out (Ten Years Later)

Ryan writes and narrates:

Mama was around for ten more years. She died in spring, her favorite time of the year. She died peacefully of natural causes while working in her garden. Everything in her garden was beautiful just like mama.
My daughters kept the garden after mama passed away like they promised her. Gardening was something my daughters did with my mom when they were growing up, and they enjoyed it as much as she did. The girls loved all the colorful flowers in mom's garden and the beautiful blue and lavender butterflies that floated in the garden during springtime.

There's also a purple and blue bird that still lands in a tree near mama's garden. My daughters nicknamed the bird blurple, because its feathers are blue and purple. Sometimes I think the bird is looking for mama. She could cheer anything up with her warm smile and songs. Rhonda said mom was like a beautiful butterfly in a garden that you want to stay forever. However, mom is no longer with us. She's gone. Oh, I miss her so much! There is no woman on this earth that will ever be able to take my mom's place. I'm so glad that my wife Lisa understands that I have love for her and my mom. She never tried to compete or make me show who I loved the most. I wish more people would understand that there is enough room in a man's heart to love both his mom and wife. The love for a mother and the love of a wife are two different types of love, and that is why a mother's love can never be replaced.

We were all sad at mom's funeral, but Calvin took it the hardest. He cried like a baby and fell to the ground calling for mama during the funeral. It was Calvin who found mom in the garden. She died in his arms.

Rhonda told Calvin that mom had made her peace with God and she wouldn't want to see us sad and crying. She gave Calvin a great big sisterly hug. Calvin wiped his tears but I could see he was still very sad and shaken. I tried to be strong, but the tears also fell from my eyes. I knew how Calvin felt, losing mom was very painful. It was one of the saddest days in my life. I felt a void in my heart. In due time God eased my pain and I too knew mom was in a better place. People came near and far to say their goodbyes to mama. Pastor Davis did the eulogy and mom's best friend Edith did the closing remarks. My niece Courtney played the piano as her sister Kelly song mom's favorite gospel song, "I'm going to see my maker." There was not a dry eye in the house.

Dad is still living. Everyone comes by the house to visit and helps him with whatever he needs. He is getting older and is now in a wheelchair.

He refuses to sell the house that he and mom shared for so many years and that he worked so hard to buy. Dad made many sacrifices and worked three jobs to pay off the family home.

I still remember how proud and happy he was when he made the final payment and received the official note from the mortgage company. He had the note framed and he and mom made a promise to each other to pass the house down through the family.

Dad said selling the house was an option that he would never consider, even if he was offered a million bucks. In fact, no amount of money would make him sell. He said the house has so many good memories of us growing up there and brings him a special joy that money could never buy. The family house is where we celebrate most of our big family events including Christmas day.

In the living room of the house is a photo collage hanging on the wall with five lavender hearts. Each of us has our own heart with our name's on it (Ryan, Rhonda, Tasha, Calvin, and Kendra) and our birth photo. In the center of the picture is a big blue heart with a photo of mom and dad. Mom is holding a purple rose in her hand that dad gave her. Every time we come over to the house dad talks about how mom treasured the collage. Sometimes he gets a little teary-eyed when he talks about the photo and mom.

Dad misses mom, but is so happy to have his family near, and we are so happy to still have him with us.

My mom always told me I was just like my dad, and that made me super proud! My dad is a man of great integrity and wisdom. He will always be my hero. Some people have a mentor or mentors. I have a dadtor. My father is my dadtor, the person I look up to. He taught and helped me with so much. Some people help you because they have interior motives or they want something from you. Some want money or favors. My dad helps me simply because I am his son, and he loves me.

I am so lucky and grateful that I had a chance to tell and show my parents how much I loved them, and so did my three sisters Kendra, Tasha, and Rhonda. My brother Calvin was given a second chance to let my mom know how much he loved and appreciated her before she passed away. He continues to now appreciate, honor, and celebrate our wonderful dad.

I knew for sure I wouldn't go to my grave with regrets. I honored my parents while they were living and didn't wait to do it through a eulogy.

I'll never forget the look on their faces the day we rented out the theater for them. My mom and dad sat in the front row holding hands like a king and queen all dressed in purple. They both had great big smiles on their faces as we honored them on stage.

My little sister Kendra planned the whole thing since she knew how much mom loved the theater. I sung, and my wife played the piano. I did poetry and so did Tasha and Rhonda. Kendra did a beautiful ballet/jazz routine. It was a fantastic evening.

The bible says that we shall honor thy mother and father so that our days may be long. In fact, to honor thy mother and father is one of the Ten Commandments. I was lucky and blessed to honor them both.

Family may not always be perfect, but family is family. If not at peace, make peace with them before their dying day… or better yet before yours.

Ryan closes his journal. The lights fade and the scene opens up at the main family house. Everyone is there and it's Christmas day. It was a beautiful winter day! The white snow looked like soft white cotton candy falling from the sky and the snowflakes glittered like shiny bright diamonds. Ryan's father blessed the food and everyone is enjoying Christmas day. After dinner everyone gathers in the living room to hear Ryan, Calvin, Rhonda, Tasha, and Kendra sing the song "A Family's Love." After they finished singing the song, everyone gathers for a family photo. They all walk into the kitchen for more desserts except for Calvin and Ryan.

Calvin: *(Calvin looking at the family photo)* Hey, another great family photo to put on my fireplace mantle, and I have the perfect frame for it. Ryan, I vowed to never take family for granted again. You have to enjoy family, because once they're gone, they're gone! There's no time for unnecessary squabbling, throwing shade, or grudges. Man… thank you for being a wonderful brother and having patience and understanding. You never gave up on me even when I was full of myself. I had my head so high up in the clouds that I lost my grounding. I had blinders on, and you helped me take them off so I could see and appreciate family. You are your brother's keeper! I hope I wasn't too much of a burden.

Ryan: Calvin, remember what dad taught us when we were kids? He would say "Family is like a precious jewel, always value and take care of family." He also said "You boys lookout for each other. One of his favorite sayings was, "He ain't heavy, he's my brother." Calvin you're not a burden, you're my brother! (*Ryan Looks at Calvin and says*) We love God, we love ourselves and like a cherry on top of a sundae there's also the love, joy, and blessings of family! As mama would always say "The bond of family shall not be broken and always cherished."

The brothers embrace and the lights fade. The song "A Family's Love" is playing.

The End.

ACKNOWLEDGEMENTS

Inspirational Credits:
God
My Mother
My Father

The love and bond of family shall not be broken

I was inspired by God to write this book, so I did. Honor thy
mother and father. Appreciate the love and joy of family.
Remember the bond, uplift, and cherish family. Let there not be
chaos, belittling, or destruction of the family unit. If there are any
shortcomings pray for one another, forgive, and let there be peace
and happiness!

Discussion Questions

You may discuss or answer these questions in a group or independently.

1. In this story Ryan the main character thanks his mother and father when he receives an award. However, his brother Calvin does not acknowledge his parents with respect to the awards and accolades he received. Compare and contrast the difference between the brothers as it relates to acknowledging and thanking their parents for their awards.

2. What is the main theme of this story? Also, discuss at least one subtheme in the book.

3. What is the significance of the colors purple, blue, and lavender, and how do they relate to the author's overall message?

4. What is the rising action and climax in this story?

5. What is the resolution in this story?

6. Who was your favorite character? Explain why. Also, what part of this book can you relate to the most?

7. What is your favorite poem in this story? Discuss why.

8. Sometimes there is tension between a wife, and her husband's mother over who he loves the most. Some wives demand they come first before the mother. How do you think Calvin and Ryan handled this matter, and what is your opinion on this topic?

9. Compare and contrast Precious Won's, "My Personal Poetry Photo Book (Honoring & Celebrating Family)" with Lorraine Hansberry's, "A Raisin in the Sun." Both authors show the bond of family in their books. Describe other similarities as well as differences between the two books.

10. Compare and contrast Precious Won's poem, "A Man" with Rudyard Kipling's poem, "If." Both authors discuss the characteristics and attributes of a man. Describe other similarities as well as differences between the two poems.

"PAGE OF FAME HONORING & CELEBRATING FAMILY"

Place your favorite photos of your mom, dad, sister(s), brother(s), grandparent(s), great grandparent(s) aunt(s), uncle(s), spouse, and children. Choose how many and what pictures you like. This is a keepsake book to pass down through your family. You can also identify who is in the photo(for example, this is my grandmother) next to the photo.

In this story the character Calvin had a special photo inside a frame that said: **"My Family."** Place at least one group family photo in this book. Use the following three pages for your choice photos.

FAMILY PHOTOS

FAMILY PHOTOS

FAMILY PHOTOS

FAMILY TREE

(My Mini Tree)

This book belongs to: _____

List as many names that you know:

Paternal Grandmother_____

Paternal Great Grandmother(s)_____

Paternal Great-Great Grandmother(s)_____

Paternal Grandfather(s)_____

Paternal Great Grandfather(s)_____

Paternal Great-Great Grandfather(s)_____

Maternal Grandmother_____

Maternal Great Grandmother(s)_____

Maternal Great-Great Grandmother(s)_____

Maternal Grandfather_____

Maternal Great Grandfather(s)_____

Maternal Great-Great Grandfather(s)_____

My Mother_____

My Father_____

My Sister(s)_____

My Brother(s)_____

My Spouse_____

My Children_____

My Grandchildren_____
_____

My Great Grandchildren_____
_____

Paternal
Aunt(s)_____

Paternal
Uncle(s)_____

Maternal
Aunt(s)_____

Maternal
Uncle(s)_____

JOURNAL
(BONUS FAMILY JOURNAL)

Celebrate and honor family while they are living!

In this story Ryan and his siblings honor their mother and father while they were LIVING, at an event called, "Honoring My Parents." Sometimes people wait until a person dies before they honor, say something nice, or show appreciation. Remarks of kindness are reserved for a eulogy, as well as through reflections as a family member lies in a casket.

A eulogy is defined as a way to honor the memory of a loved one at their funeral. It's a speech or tribute expressing how much a person means to you, information about who they are and their accomplishments. In short, a eulogy is words of kindness praising someone who has died. Why wait for a funeral? Tell family members those same kind words and show them love while they are living.

In this story Calvin was given a second chance to make amends with his family and to express and show how much he loved them. Make amends with your family if possible and let there be harmony and unity.

Use the following pages in this journal to jot down your favorite family memories and events, as well as unique and special things about your family. You may also write down words of kindness to share with family members.

MY FAMILY JOURNAL
(HONORING & CELEBRATING FAMILY)

_____
_____
_____
_____
_____
_____
_____
_____
_____
_____
_____
_____
_____
_____
_____
_____
_____
_____
_____
_____
_____
_____

MY FAMILY
JOURNAL
(HONORING & CELEBRATING FAMILY)

MY FAMILY JOURNAL

(HONORING & CELEBRATING FAMILY)

_____
_____
_____
_____
_____
_____
_____
_____
_____
_____
_____
_____
_____
_____
_____
_____
_____
_____
_____
_____
_____
_____

MY FAMILY
JOURNAL
(HONORING & CELEBRATING FAMILY)

_____
_____
_____
_____
_____
_____
_____
_____
_____
_____
_____
_____
_____
_____
_____
_____
_____
_____
_____
_____
_____
_____
_____

MY FAMILY JOURNAL
(HONORING & CELEBRATING FAMILY)

_____
_____
_____
_____
_____
_____
_____
_____
_____
_____
_____
_____
_____
_____
_____
_____
_____
_____
_____
_____
_____
_____
_____
_____

MY FAMILY
JOURNAL

Use the names from your "FAMILY TREE" to share more
information to pass down as a keepsake. Special pages about
your parents and grandparents are included.

A Special Page About My Parents

My Name: (Last, First, Mi.)_____
(Maiden)_____Born:_____-_____
Place of Birth: (City, State)_____Race:_____
My Photo:

Mother's Name: (Last, First, Mi.)_____
(Maiden)_____Born:_____-_____
Place of Birth: (City, State)_____Race:_____
My Mother's Photo:

Father's Name: (Last, First, Mi.)_____
Born:_____-_____Place of Birth: (City, State)_____Race:_____
My Father's Photo:

MY FAMILY JOURNAL

A Special Page About My Grandparents

List as many names and information that you know. Include last, first, and middle name as well as city and state for place of birth.

Grandparents On My Father's Side

My Paternal Grandmother:_____
Maiden:_____Born:_____-_____Place of Birth:_____

My Grandmother's Mother:_____
Maiden:_____ Born:_____-_____Place of Birth:_____

My Grandmother's Father:_____
Born:_____-_____Place of Birth:_____

My Paternal Grandfather:_____
Born:_____-_____Place of Birth:_____

My Grandfather's Mother:_____
Maiden: _____Born:_____-_____Place of Birth:_____

My Grandfather's Father:_____
Born:_____-_____Place of Birth:_____

Grandparents On My Mother's Side

My Maternal Grandmother:_____
Maiden:_____Born:_____-_____Place of Birth:_____

My Grandmother's Mother:_____
Maiden:_____Born:_____-_____Place of Birth:_____

My Grandmother's Father:_____
Born:_____-_____Place of Birth:_____

My Maternal Grandfather:_____
Born:_____-_____Place of Birth:_____

My Grandfather's Mother:_____
Maiden: _____Born:_____-_____Place of Birth:_____

My Grandfather's Father:_____
Born:_____-_____Place of Birth:_____

My Favorite Poems

"MY PERSONAL POETRY PHOTO BOOK"
Get Book #1 #2 and #3

My Favorite Two Poems

"My Personal Poetry Photo Book #1"

1._____
2._____

"My Personal Poetry Photo Book #2"

1._____
2._____

"My Personal Poetry Photo Book #3"

1._____
2._____

Leave reviews and comments about your favorite poems as well as chances to win free prizes and giveaways by subscribing to:
"The Precious Won Poetry Show" on YouTube
@ThePreciousWonPoetryShow

You can also go online where you purchased this book and leave a review of your favorite two poems from each book in this series.

****

Get an Autograph Copy of this book:

Author's Autograph: _____
Bring your books to one of my events for an
opportunity to get my autograph.

About The Author

Precious has received several accolades for her poetry including the prestigious Jessie Redmon Fauset Book Award for "Emotion SuperMarket A Series of Poetry." She is also the recipient of the True Boardman Award for her speech on peace and social justice. Precious is a versatile and prolific author, but writing poetry is her favorite! She has been writing poetry since the age of 12.

She is the author of the book series "Queendom Beautiful Women," "Emotion SuperMarket A Series of Poetry," "Sunshine, Flowers & The In Between," and "My Personal Poetry Photo Book." Precious' poetry books are written in a unique way, instead of turning pages reading one poem after another, her poetry aligns around a central theme and characters which includes a short story. The poetry and accompanying storyline in her books are conducive to theater and may be performed as a live play. Precious' books are never one-sided and shows both the good and bad, as well as different views and opinions.

Precious illustrates, and designs her colorful book covers that often coincide with her book themes. Her colorful book covers and thoughtful poetry has been praised by many and includes life situations that people can relate to and enjoy. Her poetry has been labeled as inspirational, thought-provoking, and heartfelt.

She earned her degree from the University of Southern California (USC) and is a native of Los Angeles. Additionally, she is a motivational speaker and is known for her famous inspirational poems "Mission Failed," "Who Really Won the Prize," "Putting On My Crown," "Don't Give Up," "Show Some Respect," and

"I'm Right Here." Her poem, "I Made My Peace With God" is also a favorite by many of her readers. Precious' poetry is relatable, understandable, inspirational, powerful, and compassionate. Her writing style and ability to connect with her readers and audience has many referring to her as "The People's Poet."

Precious' talent to connect with the audience has resulted in multiple standing ovations during her live performances, and her poetry has been featured on greeting card scrolls in Hallmark Stores. The author also toured with a performing arts group. Her favorite role was Queen Cleopatra. Besides her first love for writing, Precious has a diverse background in the arts which includes acting, dancing, and singing. Her artistic roots began at Marla Gibb's CrossRoads Arts Academy and Theater in Los Angeles. At an early age Precious was exposed to the arts by her parents and was mentored by Angela Gibbs who recognized her writing abilities and acting skills as a young teenager.

Precious is also a trained vocalist and studied dance under several instructors. She does dance choreography and is a freelance songwriter. She has a fashion background and was a model and buyer for Real Deal Clothing and Jewelry line. Additionally, she has a strong love and passion for music. When she is not writing she enjoys family time, the beach, football, having lunch with friends, listening, and playing the piano, as well as teaching acting and vocal classes. Additionally, she enjoys comedy and believes that laughter is medicine for the soul.

This author does the majority of her writing during spring which is her favorite time of the year and adores her garden that includes beautiful arrays of flowers, which she personally planted and cares for. Her colorful flowers that bloom so elegantly during the spring, the beautiful weather and of course her favorite coffee accounts for her burst of writing during the spring season.

Precious is a strong advocate of education and encourages literacy. Visit her website for upcoming performances and book signing dates at: Preciouswontheauthor.com

---

Honor thy mother and father and know family is important.

JOIN THE PRECIOUS WON BOOK CLUB

Precious Won has twelve books in her various poetry series. There will be a poetry book available for each month of the year. Get them all and add them to your book collection or as a gift. Her poetry series are: "Emotion SuperMarket A Series of Poetry," "Sunshine, Flowers & The In Between," and "My Personal Poetry Photo Book." Several of the books have been released and are available to purchase.

Precious' poetry books are written in a unique way, instead of turning pages reading one poem after another, her poetry intertwines around a central theme and characters which includes a short story.

Her poetry includes life situations that people can relate to and enjoy, as well as poetry that is great for everyday living! Her poetry has been labeled as inspirational, thought-provoking, and heartfelt.

Come along for the journey and join the book club. The author Precious Won surprises her readers with live readings of her poetry and has book giveaways. You can also check out her performance dates.

Join the book reading club at:
Preciouswontheauthor.com

Other Books By the Author Precious Won:

<u>EMOTION SUPERMARKET A SERIES POETRY</u>
1. "Emotion SuperMarket A Series of Poetry (Book #1)"

2. "Emotion SuperMarket A Series of Poetry (Book #2)"

3. "Emotion SuperMarket A Series of Poetry (Book #3)"

<u>QUEENDOM BEAUTIFUL WOMEN</u>
4. "Queendom Beautiful Women (Book #1)"

5. "Queendom Beautiful Women (Book #2)"

6. "Queendom Beautiful Women (Book #3)"

<u>SUNSHINE, FLOWERS & THE IN BETWEEN</u>
7. "Sunshine, Flowers & The In Between - Book #1 (Inspiration and Hope)"

8. "Sunshine, Flowers & The In Between - Book #2 (Love and Second Chances)"

9. "Sunshine, Flowers & The In Between - Book #3 (Peace and Happiness)"

<u>MY PERSONAL POETRY PHOTO BOOK</u>
10. *"My Personal Poetry Photo Book #1 (Honoring & Celebrating Family)"

11. "My Personal Poetry Photo Book #2 (Sisters)"

12. "My Personal Poetry Photo Book #3 (Siblings)"

www.ingramcontent.com/pod-product-compliance
Lightning Source LLC
LaVergne TN
LVHW021520080426
835509LV00018B/2567